The Golden Age Of
Steam
IN PICTURES

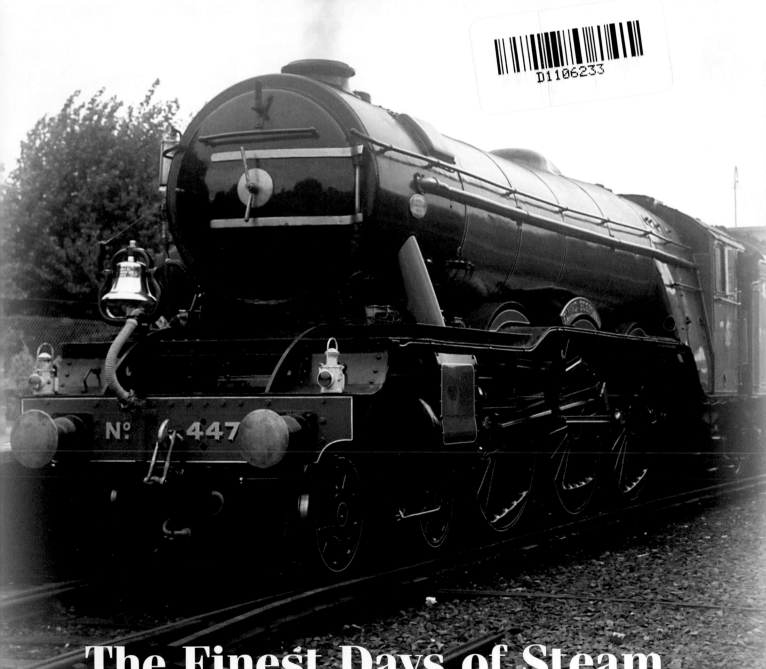

No. 447

The Finest Days of Steam

Contents

STEAM

28

44

First published in the UK in 2012

© Instinctive Product Development 2013

This edition published by Park Lane Books

www.parklanebooksltd.vpweb.co.uk

Printed in China

ISBN: 978-1-906969-43-1

Designed by: BrainWave

Creative Director: Kevin Gardner

Written by: Jessica Toyne

Images courtesy of PA Photos

The Story of Steam

The ability to move equipment by steam power alone has been known for hundreds of years. But this was not made practical until the 1700s when a number of different machines were made to pump out excess water from mines. These engines worked by condensing steam into water and using a partial vacuum to draw water along a pipe. As a result steam power was finally born.

It is a popular belief that the world's first steam locomotive was Stephenson's Rocket, which was first unveiled in 1829. In truth, it was Cornishman Richard Trevithick who made the first example of a steam locomotive 25 years earlier in 1804. However, this was not the start of Trevithick's steam story. In 1801, he built the first steam 'road' locomotive aptly named the "Puffing Devil" which he launched on a site in Camborne, Cornwall, which today is known as Fore Street. Leading onto Camborne Hill, the mining engineer drove his engine up the hill and it is this surprising sight that is rumoured to have led to the Cornish folksong, *Going Up Camborne Hill, Coming Down*. However, the engine proved of little practical value as it was unable to sustain sufficient steam pressure for long. Undeterred, the Cornishman had already taken out a patent for his high pressure steam engine in 1802.

The most early railway locomotives were organised into classes with each one having their own specific design and role. Many of these locomotives were also given codes representing their different wheel arrangements. The traditional railway track design was made to support and guide the locomotive at high speeds.

As far back as ancient Greece, carts that were pulled by horses would often leave tracks along the dirt roads. Greek statesman, Pericles, began making tracks out of stone to help transport heavier loads over greater distances. This idea soon spread across Europe and the UK where different areas adopted wooden railways during the reign of Elizabeth I. This practice gradually evolved into the use of railroad cars that were pulled along by horses in and around the coalmines of England. By the year 1630, the system of using wagons and carts with iron wheels on wooden tracks was a common sight. Although these were still pulled along by horses, this new innovation in transport was deemed to have considerable advantages in traversing slopes and manoeuvring over rough terrain. Throughout the 1600s wooden railways were very commonly used. Later during the 1700s, especially in iron mining areas, wooden railways were beginning to be replaced with iron ones which were perceived to do the job more effectively; it was discovered that heavier loads could be transported more easily.

■ **RIGHT:** Painting of Richard Trevithick.
■ **FAR RIGHT:** Trevithick's Steam Circus.

■ **ABOVE:** Locomotion No. 1 at the 1925 anniversary celebrations.

■ **RIGHT:** Sir Isaac Newton.

The first public railway in the world was the Surrey Iron Railway, which linked the former towns of Surrey and Wandsworth. The railway was first opened in 1803 and used a horse-drawn service, which was initially dedicated for goods. Users had to provide their own horses and wagons, paying a fee to use the railway (tram road).

One of the pioneers of steam was Sir Isaac Newton who helped develop the idea of a kettle on wheels that could be propelled by its own steam. Frenchman, Nicolas Cugnot, then produced a very basic tractor, which could move itself along by its own steam power. However, it was Richard Trevithick who proved to be the main pioneer of steam with the introduction of his steam engine.

Richard Trevithick was a British inventor and mining engineer. Being described by his schoolmaster as "obstinate and inattentive" Trevithick learnt his skills from an early age in the Cornish tin mines. He began by experimenting with a variety of different steam-driven models before designing the world's first full-scale steam engine. The Penydarren tram road engine as it was known first ran on 21 February 1804, hauling 10 tons of iron and 70 men nearly 10 miles from Penydarren Ironworks in South Wales at a speed of 5mph. At the time though, Trevithick's engine seemed little more than a novelty to critics. Even so, several of Trevithick's locomotives went on to be built as small, high pressure stationary engines. One of these engines was presented in Tyneside, Newcastle where a young George Stephenson took a great interest in its design. During 1807 the first passenger railway opened in South Wales, using horse-drawn carts

with fare-paying passengers.

George Stephenson designed his first locomotive in September 1825. Aptly called, Locomotion No. 1, it was designed specifically for the Stockton to Darlington Railway. The Locomotion's engine had a rather complicated drive system, which used vertical cylinders connected to all four wheels. However, the design was largely ineffective as it only had a small single flue boiler. Later in 1829, Stephenson introduced the Rocket, which represented a major leap forward in locomotive design. It had a number of new features following on from Stephenson's first design and formed the standard of almost all steam locomotives that were to follow. The Rocket introduced the

■ **ABOVE:** James May with a replica of "Rocket".
■ **RIGHT:** George Stephenson.

first ever passenger service, which was remarkable at a time where many thought steam-powered engines could not be achieved. The Rocket represented a revolution in travel and was reported on the front page of newspapers all around the world. It could reach up to 37mph and interest was so high that around 15,000 people came to watch it during its Rainhill trials.

In the same year that the Rocket was introduced, John Braithwaite and John Ericsson designed the Novelty. This engine also took part in the Rainhill trials and helped push forward a new concept of locomotive design. Although it never proved as successful as Stephenson's Rocket, it employed two vertical cylinders and was the first locomotive to use a double cranked axle.

After the success of Stephenson's Rocket, the Patent Engine was introduced in 1833. The pace and development of engines at this time was very quick and within a few years Stephenson's Patent Engine was being built by manufacturers all around the world. It had a long boiler design, which included larger, horizontal cylinders, which drove two pairs of linked wheels through a cranked axle. It also included a full smoke box and protective buffers that were located at the front of the engine.

In the early 1830s the Liverpool and Manchester Railway was the first line to introduce two-way running tracks, railway stations, timetables and basic signalling. Many of these things are now taken for granted on the modern railways but originated well over a hundred years previously. The first signalling was done by hand either using flags or lamps at night. In the 1840s the semaphore

- **OPPOSITE INSET**: Commerative 200 year steam anniversary £2 coin.
- **OPPOSITE:** A steam locomotive explosion, c1850.
- **ABOVE:** Inaugural journey of the Liverpool and Manchester Railway, c1830.
- **BELOW:** GWR Firefly reconstruction at Didcot Railway Centre.

flagging system was adapted and used widely on all railways. Boards were also used by signalmen, which were vertically pivoted using red lamps at night to represent stop and a white light for all clear. Green lamps were initially used to tell drivers to "approach with caution" but this later changed to mean "all clear" or "go". At this time railway travel was regarded as rather safe as the locomotive speeds were relatively low. Even though the railway was not a particularly fast way of travelling about, it had an enormous affect on the world, opening up

a great deal of new possibilities that people had previously thought were never possible.

In 1840 Great Western Railway (GWR) introduced the Firefly Class 2-2-2. Stephenson's Rocket had started a flurry of development from other manufacturers all over the world that were eager to produce the fastest and most powerful locomotives. Many of the engines of this time used Stephenson's early designs with a long, multi tube boiler, inside cylinders driving onto a cranked wheel spindle. Engines also began using cylinder valves that could allow the steam cut-off positions to be adjusted. The Firefly had a very smooth and stable ride largely thanks to the use of GWR's broad track gauge. It could reach speeds of over 60mph and in 1844 completed a run between

London and Exeter in four hours and 30 minutes.

The railways across the UK and Europe usually began by following old and established trade routes, linking cities, towns and industrial businesses together. In the US the railway offered people a whole new world of possibilities and as the railway network was developed, many towns and cities were initially founded by those pioneering the railways. Many cities we know today including Atlanta, Atlantic City and Anchorage were all built by these early American railway pioneers.

After the success of the Liverpool and Manchester Railway, it brought about a whole new network of lines that began running from London. These included lines to Birmingham, Bristol, Southampton, Manchester,

■ **BELOW:** A locomotive designed by Crampton, c1846.

Edinburgh and Glasgow. People's lives were changing forever due to the railway networks and by the 1850s London was beginning to receive goods from Burton on Trent, Yorkshire and as far afield as the Scottish Highlands.

This new age of steam enabled industries to grow and reach new heights of development. Raw material could be sourced and sent to the manufacturer and then on to the customer much more quickly and cheaply. People found that they were no longer restricted to their small local towns and were free to explore and visit different areas of the country with relative ease.

Steam locomotives could be grouped into a number of basic categories according to the duties they were designed to perform. In the order of evolution these include, industrial, freight, express, passenger, shunting, suburban and cross-country.

By 1852 the Crampton 4-2-0 was the latest locomotive to be introduced. The initial demand for faster engines required even bigger boilers and wheels. The problem with this was the bigger the wheels an engine had, the higher the boiler's centre of gravity, making it much more unstable at higher speeds. T R Crampton presented an effective solution, which used a single pair of driving wheels at the rear of the engine and four smaller wheels at the front to carry the load of the boiler. This design became particularly popular in France throughout the century. By 1870 the Crampton model was modified and broke the world speed record setting a top speed of 89.5mph while pulling 157 tons.

The American Type 4-4-0 was introduced in the US in 1855. The railways in the US were developed

■ **RIGHT:** Ffestiniog Railway's first Double Fairlie locomotive "Little Wonder" with long goods train, 1871.

slightly differently to the European tracks, as their engineers had to compete with much steeper gradients and severe curves. As a result the US locomotives were designed to be more flexible and therefore used four-wheel swivelling wheel trucks, which were also known as bogies. These early steam engines burnt wood and could only manage a top speed of 40mph. However the 4-4-0 was ideally suited to the rougher tracks of the frontier lands and so the rush for speed was put on hold in order to keep building long lengths of track across the country.

The early locomotive designers felt that a single pair of driving wheels allowed for greater freedom and therefore would allow for greater speeds. More improved manufacturing materials and designs soon meant that multiple driving wheel layouts became the norm. The boilers of locomotives would soon be lowered with the use of outside cylinders. A variety of wheel configurations were tested in an attempt to find the best one. The different codes associated with locomotives were ways of determining the number of wheels they were supported by. For example, the Class 2-4-0 means that the locomotive has 2 wheels at the front and 4 wheels of a different size behind. The 0 means there are no other wheels fitted at the back of the locomotive. The last major development to locomotive power came from Wilhelm Schmidt. Located in Berlin he worked on a variety of superheaters, which could provide improvements to engine power in the early 1900s. He developed a technique that could increase the power of the engine as well as its overall efficiency. The locomotive mechanics were not complicated in any way and railway companies were soon seeing a great deal of money being saved when using these new superheaters.

The maximum speed and power of

■ **BELOW:** Great Western Railway steam locomotive "Castle" Class 4-6-0 No. 7029.

■ **ABOVE:** Left to Right: GWR King, Castle and Star Classes.

■ **BELOW:** GWR "Castle" Class 4-6-0, Rainhill Parade, 1980.

■ **ABOVE:** Side angle view of an American Class 4-8-4.

■ **LEFT:** The last ever steam engine made for the Union Pacific railroad in 1944.

an engine is very much related to how large it can be made. As the speed of locomotives gradually became larger and larger, this increase was directly linked to the build quality of the railway track and also the strength of every bridge on the line. Companies soon realised by increasing the number of axles on each locomotive this would reduce the weight each axle was subjected to. This was very important as along with the total engine weight it determined the size and performance of all new locomotives being produced. In 1926 the GWR Castle Class set an average speed world record time on a schedule service between Swindon and Paddington at 81.7mph.

The GWR Castle Class 4-6-0 was introduced in 1923. Specific clearances within the cylinders, valves or insulation all had a major effect on the amount of steam or heat that was lost while the locomotive was running. GWR were well known for their precision manufacturing and the Castle Class was to prove this after showing a 25 per cent improvement in coal used per drawbar-horsepower-hour against the standard for the day. It was claimed by many that the standard limits of some new locomotives was the same as the GWR standards when they were beginning to be worn out. Many GWR locomotives were certainly known for their reliability at the time.

The American and Canadian Class 4-8-4 were among some of the largest locomotives to go into regular service in the US. They were first introduced in 1926 and were fitted with eight driving wheels, which allowed for a very long boiler and plenty of contact to help transmit the power onto the track. Its smaller four wheels at the rear of the engine also helped to allow for a larger grate area to be built into the firebox.

Wind resistance became extremely important to locomotives, especially

when they were beginning to reach speeds of over 100mph. The Mallard previously held the record as the fastest steam locomotive in the world after reaching a top speed of 126mph. The fastest service running locomotive is set by the Silver Fox, which reached 133mph in 1936. By this time however, the days of steam were sadly coming to an end. There had been a number of serious accidents and deaths, which brought about the introduction of speed limits in an effort to stop different companies racing each

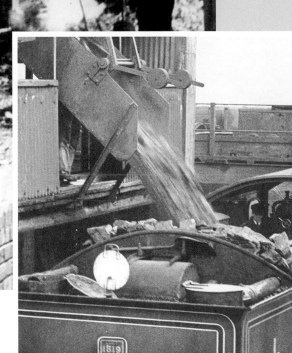

■ **ABOVE:** Royal Scot Class locomotive No. 6188 "The Girl Guide."

■ **LEFT:** Mallard gets a check from its crew, 1963.

other to claim the quickest service. In addition, the increasing efficiency of electric and diesel locomotives was another sign that steam power would soon be a thing of the past.

Steam At Work & Pleasure

A member of the Home Guard patrols on duty at a London railway terminus in July 1940 (above). The Home Guard was comprised of volunteers who were otherwise ineligible for military service due to their age or medical impediment. The defence organisation served the country between 1940 and 1944 and was tasked with protecting vital transport links such as the railways, locomotives and rolling stock from enemy sabotage. They were also

and supplies were transported to the correct places at the right time. Here, (pictured above) men are working on the boiler of a steam locomotive, one of many new trains being made to keep up with the demands of the Armed Forces.

The British government gave the order for the start of the evacuation on 31 August 1939, two days before the official declaration of war with Germany. Around 3.75 million people were transported from cities to the safer rural areas in an effort to remove them from potential target areas. This figure included more than 800,000 school children (accompanied by numerous teachers acting as their guardians) and over half a million mothers and youngsters (under the age of five). With the speed of Operation Pied Piper, it was inevitable that families were accidentally separated but the children (pictured below) are in good spirits, however, as they wave goodbye at Paddington Station before boarding a train bound for the west of England. As the anticipated bombardment had not begun by early 1940, many were returned only to be evacuated a second time with the onslaught of the Blitz in the autumn of that year.

responsible for guarding the coastal areas of Britain as well as other important places such as airfields, factories and explosives stores.

The whole country got behind the war effort after the outbreak of hostilities in September 1939. Iron and steel, however, were in high demand – due to the necessities of equipping the troops – and the government therefore took over their supply. They also took control of the railways in order to ensure that troops

Even in the traumatic years of the Second World War, Paddington was a constant hive of activity while the Underground tunnels were regularly utilised to shelter the public during Luftwaffe air raids. Despite warnings that passengers might be stranded if they travelled too far and the railway network was hit by German bombs, hordes of people were often desperate to get away from London and its dangers. Frequent trains were laid on to carry holidaymakers to resorts in the west of England. It has also been rumoured that a secret tunnel was built which linked Paddington to Buckingham Palace, thereby offering the Royal family an escape route should it be deemed necessary.

Paddington was one of the numerous stations hit by German bombs during the Second World War. The direct hits that Paddington suffered in March 1944 saw a 40-foot wide and 12-foot deep crater appear in the area that platforms six and seven had previously occupied. Once the air raid had finished, workmen were quickly detailed to

clear the rubble in order to restore service to the lines. Amazingly, they achieved this the same day, with all obstructing material being removed by the evening.

It was not the first time that Paddington had suffered at the hands of the Luftwaffe; high explosive bombs hit the station during the Blitz in October 1940 causing multiple fatalities and the suspension of services between Edgware Road and South Kensington. The main station building itself had been designed by Isambard Kingdom Brunel and was opened in May 1854. The famed engineer revolutionised public transport with his ingenious bridges and tunnels and oversaw the construction of Britain's first railway, the Great Western Railway, in the 1830s and 1840s.

While Underground stations had been used as unofficial air raid shelters during the first global conflict, the government actively opposed the idea as the Second World War approached. They were, it seemed, worried that Londoners would develop a "deep shelter mentality" and refuse to come back to the surface.

In the mid-19th Century, comfort largely depended upon which class the passengers were travelling in. First class was more often than not quite lavish and luxurious while second class was understandably much sparser as the cost of travel was cheaper. Third class, however, was a real test of endurance and passengers would often just hope to stay dry and pray that any delays were short so that the ordeal couldn't get any worse. It wasn't until basic facilities were introduced during the 1870s that conditions began to improve and it was the London and North Western Railway who were the first to introduce toilets in its sleeper cars. The first dining car was in place by the end of 1879 on the Great

Northern Railway – running between London Kings Cross and Leeds – although the entire carriage was separated from the remainder of the train to make it more exclusive.

Pictured below is the interior of a new first-class restaurant car on the Great Northern Railways service between London and Leeds in January 1903. It is obviously aimed at the more affluent passengers and the introduction of the notorious British Rail sandwich is still a long way off…

By the mid-1930s, rail journeys had become a more sociable event as these Christmas revellers (overleaf) on a London, Midland and Scottish Railway service demonstrate. The Railways Act of 1921 had forced the merger of more than 120 companies into just four as the government sought to make the railways more efficient and cost-effective.

By the 1950s, following nationalisation of the railways, the British Transport Hotel and Catering Services were offering more affordable refreshments such as Packed Meals (2/6), Tray Meals (3/6) and Compact Meal Boxes (7/6).

The locomotive driver had one of the most important roles to play in the history of steam, yet more often than not – despite being an integral figure, beyond the railway staff – he was largely unseen and was defined by his locomotive. Indeed, he was barely thought of by many of the fare-paying public throughout the latter part of the 19th Century unless something was wrong. However, despite being taken for granted – to an extent – and little understood, the driver was at the heart of the railway and its workings and had a crucial and vital role to play.

The driver had overall responsibility for the locomotive and was in charge of controlling the engine's starts, stops and speed. He was supported by a fireman responsible for the fuel for the fire, the steam pressure and water levels in the boiler as well as the storage tanks. In fact, the pressure for the fireman was immense and the job proved to be extremely labour intensive to say the least. Although firemen were employed by the Royal Navy and other industries, they were generally known as stokers. However, it is on the railways with which firemen are largely associated. It was usually their job to clean the ash and dust from the boiler before lighting the fire. They would then add water to the boiler and ensure that there was sufficient fuel for the journey. The fire would then be lit and it would be back-breaking work to ensure that the raising or banking of the fire was at a level appropriate for the speed of the locomotion. This would be carried out on instruction from the driver (also known as an engineer in the US). Mechanical stokers were eventually installed in the larger steam locomotives as a way to ease pressure on the fireman. It worked through a screw conveyor which was driven by an auxiliary steam engine, feeding coal into the

firebox. The fuel was then disbursed across the grate by steam jets, which the fireman would control. However, many firemen saw their time in the cab as an apprenticeship which would one day lead them to the top job – as driver.

There was a huge attraction to becoming a locomotive driver. When the railway was new and exciting, there were many small boys who dreamed of one day becoming part of the hub of the railway. It also follows that many working-class children during the latter part of the 19th Century and early part of the 20th Century would pick a particular occupation; there was the sea, armed forces, teaching and nursing (for girls), but the job of locomotive driver was high up on the list. The appeal of the job was direct and practical and had, with it, a mystery besides the good pay, job security and status. Added to which, the locomotive was noisy, dramatic, powerful and intriguing and the job of driver was seen as exciting and heroic. The engine itself had a large part to play in tempting young men into the cab – there was something exhilarating about the sheer size of the locomotive, its power and speed and the fact that it relied so heavily on pure elements of water and fire. It was, above all, an occupation of which to be proud.

Drivers and firemen didn't operate on their own, however, and the guard, conductor and station staff were instrumental in keeping up a good reputation amongst the general public. Working for the railway was more than just a job; it became a way of life.

Poverty was still rife throughout the latter part of the 19th Century and many ordinary families were unable to afford the time or money to travel. However, weekends away and holidays for a longer duration were becoming the norm for middle-class families across the UK during the late 1800s and, by the 1920s and 1930s, travel was becoming more affordable to the masses. Major cities were the first to catch on and the development of the railways during the Victorian era helped to promote and encourage tourism (in its infancy) to the wider general public.

Railway staff were the mainstay of the competing companies and

reputation was everything. The Station Master was in charge and the most visible member of staff on the station, offering advice and answering the queries of anxious passengers. It was here that holidaymakers were given their first impression of the company that would be transporting them to relaxing breaks away from the humdrum of life. It meant time away from often cramped, industrial conditions and various destinations including Cleethorpes, Skegness, Clacton-on-Sea and Blackpool became popular resorts with those from the cities. However, holidays were not necessarily "paid" by employers as they are today and

– until the 1930s – taking time off work often meant going without pay. But, things were changing and many employers began to realise that providing paid holiday time was beneficial to their workforce. In addition, for some industries, shutdown at certain points of the year was crucial for essential maintenance and it was then that workers were able to "get away" for a short time. It is also known that "orchestrated absenteeism" in some industrial towns was evident and many workers took the opportunity to take an excursion.

In 1938, the Holidays with Pay Act changed things for good and established that paid leave was justifiable. The Act didn't cover many issues such as how many consecutive days a worker could have as holiday, however, it was a first important step and the railway provided a lifeline to those who could afford to get away from it all.

But even though employers agreed to paid leave and the railways gladly

transported holidaymakers, it was still expensive to find somewhere to stay, especially in seaside resorts. Some families would take advantage of renting a plotland bungalow which in effect meant that they could buy a piece of land that had been divided into plots and build a holiday home or smallholding. Many plotlands were rented out to families seeking a break away from the city. That great British holiday institution, the holiday camp, came into its own during the post-war years and the railways played an integral part in shifting the millions of holidaymakers. Pictured above a huge crowd say "Bye-di-bye" to Butlins Filey Holiday Camp in the summer of 1947 as a Thomson Class B1 arrives to load passengers.

Entrepreneur William "Billy" Butlin came up with the idea following a visit to Canada during the First World War when he had seen lakeside holiday centres. He decided to introduce them to the British and sited his first camp in the seaside town of Skegness. It opened in April 1936 and was basic, to say the least, with guests staying in prefabricated chalets and taking their meals in a canteen. Disappointed that his guests stayed in their family groups and were reluctant to mingle with other holidaymakers, Butlin introduced his now famous Red Coats to organise events and entertainment.

The Skegness camp had been commandeered by the Royal Navy during the Second World War and only reopened in May 1946 boasting new facilities such as swimming pools, tennis courts, a ballroom and theatre.

Preserved Railways

The advent of new engines, in the guise of diesel and electric trains, swiftly saw the demise of steam during the first half of the 20th Century. But, in some areas of the globe, steam held on. Today, there are stunning scenic journeys to be taken by steam and many railways have been steadfastly preserved by enthusiastic volunteers who refuse to let the story of steam disappear altogether from the pages of history.

Preserving a railway for steam locomotion is a time consuming and costly business, especially in today's environment where specialist machinery and infrastructure are needed to ensure that lines are able to keep going. The engines themselves also contribute to the hard work with constant maintenance, primitive tools and working parts. It takes hours to "boil up" a steam locomotive before it is operational and water and large amounts of fuel are essential to the running of the engine. At the end of the day, clearing all the industrial waste generated by these engines is just as labour intensive as running them on a journey, so the dedication and hard graft that goes into providing thousands of people across the globe with a chance to experience the "glory days" should not be underestimated.

Bluebell Railway

The year 2010 marked the 50th anniversary of the much-loved Bluebell Railway in the heart of Sussex. It was reopened, following the demise of branch lines, in 1960 and is one of the oldest preserved railways in the UK today. To mark the anniversary, an appeal is currently under way to keep the line running smoothly that includes a proposal for a pioneer heritage railway connected to the national network with a platform at East Grinstead station. The railway is renowned for its care of the environment and is anxious to provide benefits across the local community. The project requires £3.5 million to be able to complete its objectives which would benefit the environment from reduced pollution from cars, provide conservation for wildlife, an increase in local employment, provide education and training and would contribute to the region's tourism and economy.

The Bluebell Railway is situated in the Sussex Weald near the Ashdown Forest and offers all volunteers the opportunity to drive a train by working their way up through the ranks of cleaner, fireman, passed fireman and driver. The line is currently nine miles long running between Sheffield Park, near Brighton and Kingscote, but with the anniversary appeal it is hoped to extend the line to East Grinstead by a further two miles. During May, bluebells through the wooded part of the journey are bountiful and it is from these tiny wild flowers that the railway takes its name. The train then travels through Horsted Keynes – where the working sheds are located – before heading north to Sharpthorne Tunnel. This is the longest tunnel on a preserved line in the UK at 710 metres. The train then reaches its destination in Kingscote. The first ever line here opened in

1882 on the London Brighton and South Coast Railway. Gradients on the line can range up to 1-in-75 which is a challenge for the railway's smaller engines and the climb lasts for several miles. There are currently around 30 locomotives associated with the Bluebell Railway and many of them are still working. Some engines, however, are undergoing a service at any one time.

Interestingly, in keeping with the train's age and heritage, the railway offers first- and third-class tickets to its passengers. There are some beautifully restored first-class carriages for those passengers seeking slightly more comfort, while third class offers the chance to experience the coaches as they would have been during their heyday. True to form, the railway still also uses working wagons, which would have been much more prevalent during the age of steam on the Bluebell Railway than passenger trains.

Paignton & Dartmouth Steam Railway

Owned by the Dartmouth Steam Train and River Boat Company, the Paignton & Dartmouth Steam Railway takes passengers on a journey from Paignton in Devon, along the cliffs overlooking Torbay on a spectacular trip before reaching its final destination on the River Dart. The line was reopened by the Dart Valley Railway in 1972 – which was in fact, the same year it had been closed by the government following the Beeching Report in the 1960s. The journey today consists of breathtaking scenery along the English Riviera coastline. First, the train reaches the picturesque station at Churston which is situated on the main road to the small fishing port of Brixham. Opened in March 1861, the station was first named Brixham Road. Having changed its name to Churston it was sold to the Dart

Valley Railway in 1972 and became an important centre for engineering – despite its scenic surroundings. From here, the train then travels through the woodland known as Long Wood which borders the Dart Estuary before finally reaching Kingswear. The area is renowned for its birds and sea life along with other wildlife including herons, kingfishers, buzzards, dolphins and seals. This brings the railway towards its final destination at the edge of the River Dart. The Dartmouth Steam Train and River Boat Company now offer passengers a 20 per cent discount in conjunction with English Heritage so that visitors and passengers may take the opportunity to visit Dartmouth Castle which was the first English castle to boast guns as its main armament. In addition, the company also offer other trips which can be combined with a trip on the railway. In 2010, passengers were offered the opportunity to take a full day excursion from Torquay to Dartmouth by boat with a return trip by steam train to Paignton (and a short bus journey back to Torquay). This combined day out gives the chance to relax and enjoy the English Riviera along the South Devon coastline to Dartmouth before returning on the foot passenger ferry from Dartmouth to Kingswear. From here, the steam train transports passengers to Paignton where they catch the bus which departs every 15 minutes. The Sea Train runs between May and June on a selected timetable. There are also certain days of operation throughout September, however it runs everyday between the beginning of July and end of August.

Brecon Mountain Railway

The Brecon Mountain Railway started life as an industrial hub serving the iron works and mines in this area of Wales. The first yards of the line follow a new alignment cut through rock on a narrow gauge, but the original line joins this from the right. From here, passengers can see the river Taf Fechan as well as industrial heritage. While up in the hills beyond the gorge, Vaynor Quarry is still visible and is, incidentally, the site where most of the ballast for the railway was taken. The journey then continues forward across the valley where the small village of Pontsticill can be seen before the train enters a cutting. Streams moving swiftly down the rocky terrain are also visible before reaching the Taf Fechan Reservoir which provides a spectacular backdrop along with the three peaks of the Brecon Beacons. The left peak, Corn Du, sits neatly next to the middle peak, Pen-Y-Fan, which is the highest

in South Wales at 2,906 feet, while to the right is Y Cribyn. The train then travels into the Brecon Beacons National Park where a disused felt works can be seen.

The Reservoir Dam comes into view at about the time the journey descends on Pontsticill Station. Completed in 1927, the reservoir holds up to 3,400 million gallons of water and became infamous when it flooded Capel Taf Fechan, a 15th-Century chapel and the local vicarage as well as Bethlehem Congregational Chapel, a number of cottages, small holdings and land that belonged to eight neighbouring farms. In fact in times of drought some of the remains of these old

buildings can be seen above water level. Without stopping, the train moves swiftly on its journey along the banks of the reservoir and for a short distance, the train moves away from the original line to avoid the Merthyr Tydfil Sailing Club. By the time the journey is drawing to its end, the train has reached the northern end of the reservoir where the locomotive is then changed to the other end of the carriages for the return journey. Unlike the outward journey, the train stops at Pontsticill Station on the way back, offering passengers the opportunity to relax and catch a later train back to the first destination, or to do some walking in picturesque surroundings.

North Yorkshire Moors Railway

North Yorkshire Moors Railway, or NYMR as it's more commonly known, provides a great family day out and combines the world's only steam passenger bus – the "Elizabeth", sponsored by the railway – with steam train operations. The company's Goathland station enjoys celebrity status with links to *Heartbeat* and *Harry Potter*. Travelling through the rugged Dales, it is possible to make a request for the train to stop at the tiny picturesque halt of Newton Dale which gives passengers access to the nearby National Park. This is a perfect point to take a walk and enjoy the spectacular wildlife. Levisham is the NYMR's station in a 1912 style and is accessible from only one road on a solitary hill surrounded by the glorious Yorkshire Moors. More information can be gained from the Levisham Station Group website. Pickering is the perfect start to an exciting steam adventure. The station boasts smart 1930s decoration and the village is well worth exploring. The station is also home to traditional tea rooms which offer freshly baked produce throughout the day.

NYMR offer passengers an on board magnificent Pullman service with a magical setting. The carriages denote a bygone era with lavish decoration and events are regular on this exquisite train service. Most are in operation throughout the year at weekends and in June, Saturday nights are especially dedicated to a special time on the themed murder mystery trains. There is a festive train at Christmas.

Stunning Scenic Journeys

Steam is powerful and exciting and from North and South America, to Europe, Africa, Asia and Australia it is possible to experience travelling by steam. The Pride of Africa offers passengers a number of different journeys from Pretoria to Mafeking, on the Zambezi Steam Express, and from Cape Town to Dar es Salaam, while in Europe travel is offered on the Trans-Siberian Express, the Danube Express and, of course, one of the most luxurious trains of all time, the Orient Express. The Shangri-La Express in Asia is renowned for being the most modern hotel train in China and combined with a Three-Gorges cruise is noted as one of the best ways to discover the country. In the UK, steam travel is possible across the country from the Highlands of Scotland, through Yorkshire and across Wales, and down to Cornwall in the South West. Engines and carriages have been painstakingly and lovingly restored wherever steam travel is found.

The name the Orient Express has long been associated with one of the world's most luxurious and exclusive trains. The Venice Simplon-Orient Express is one of the most famous across the globe and is renowned for its original 1920s carriages carrying passengers from city to city throughout Europe with their Lalique glass panels and Art Deco delights. Offering the chance to travel in elegant style, the train boasts a strong tradition with the past and each individual carriage has a history of its own and has long been crossing between London and Paris and continental Europe. Today, there are numerous journeys available and many visitors to Europe choose this train to cement their holiday on the continent. Many opt for the London/Paris to Venice route which can be taken in either direction while others may choose to travel from Venice itself to various locations including Prague, Rome, Vienna, Budapest and Istanbul.

Passengers taking any journey on the Orient Express are assigned a dedicated cabin steward who may be called at any time of the day or night. The steward is supported by many other staff, including the Maître d' and train manager.

Moving to Scotland, steam passengers in the Highlands may experience the Findhorn Viaduct on the main Perth to Inverness railway around 14 miles (22 km) southeast of Inverness. The curved viaduct sits impressively surveying the valley of the River Findhorn some 49 m or 160 feet below and is around 400 m (438 yards) in length. The grand design consists of nine lattice-steel structures which are supported by stone piers. It was built between 1894 and 1897 by Sir John Fowler and Murdoch Paterson. The Britannia Class Locomotive 70013, shown in the picture crossing the Findhorn Viaduct, is one of only two surviving engines of its type. Known as the Oliver Cromwell, the engine led the Great Britain III Excursion from Bristol to Preston and Exeter St David's before crossing the Highlands in this memorable steam adventure.

The longest and most famous viaduct on the Settle – Carlisle Railway is the Ribblehead Viaduct in North Yorkshire crossing the River Ribble valley. Surrounded by spectacular scenic beauty, the viaduct, like the Findhorn Viaduct is curved and this enables passengers to see various other parts of the train (and engine) as it curves its way across the river some 32 m (404 feet) below. The first stone of engineer John Sydney Crossley's viaduct was laid on 12 October 1870. The impressive construction took four years to build and spans 402 m or 440 yards with 24 arches to support its infrastructure.

The Glacier Express is often advertised as "the world's slowest express train" travelling through some of Europe's most beautiful and untouched scenery in the Alpine countryside. Crossing over mountain streams with their "roaring" waters and passing by towering mountainsides, the journey between St Moritz and Zermatt – both high points themselves – is a seven and a half hour ride comprising 291 bridges and 91 tunnels through unspoilt panoramic scenery from Davos, near St Moritz, the highest altitude town in Europe, to the home of the Matterhorn. The towns are connected by the UNESCO World Heritage Railway and the line also runs through the "Grand Canyon" of Switzerland, the Rheinschlucht Gorge. Passengers are treated to lunch in the dining car with their own window seat and are encouraged to take in the Landwasser Viaduct, the Oberalp Pass as well as the famous Furka Tunnel. The train operates during the summer months and the journey makes brief stops at Chur and Brig on both the inward and outward journeys.

The Georgetown Loop Railroad in the Colorado Rockies actively encourages its passengers to "taste their way around the world" with wine tasting and hors d'oeuvres. Each train journey is a chance to sample wines from across the globe while experiencing the true history of North American steam against the stunning backdrop of the Colorado Rockies. The Railroad brings Colorado's history to the present day as the train pulls up Clear Creek Canyon, past a steep history of gold and silver mining along the way. Trains depart from Devil's Gate Station in Georgetown or Silver Plume Depot (during season only) and there are enclosed and open carriages for passengers to enjoy on this scenic route.

The longest railway in the world is the Trans-Siberian Railway which takes 14 days across two continents and seven different time zones. Alongside the Orient Express, the Trans-Siberian is one of the most famous in the world, on board a private train called the Golden Eagle. Many of the days throughout the two weeks are given over to passengers to tour cities along the route and the tour offers three days relaxing on the train itself. This exclusive journey has highlights which include a Mongolia visit and an outdoor train ride at Lake Baikal followed by a beach picnic before exploring Siberian wooden architecture. This is an exciting and interesting way to experience the vastness of Siberia travelling between Moscow and Vladivostok in either direction.

One of the most important UK journeys is on the Jacobite Steam Train, which passes from Fort William to the fishing port of Mallaig. Passing Ben Nevis, before it reaches further towards the Road to the Isles, the train crosses the Glenfinnan Viaduct, where imposing arches support the railway across the glen to Glenfinnan Station.

The line here originally stretched from Glasgow to Fort William where it was finished in 1894. The journey is renowned for its beautiful countryside which is lost to those travelling via road. The line eventually reached Mallaig in 1901 and the viaduct – built of concrete by Robert McAlpine (Concrete Bob) – is 1,000 feet long and 100 feet high.

It is reported that no visit to North Wales should be undertaken without a ride on the narrow gauge railway between Porthmadog and Blaenau Ffestiniog. The railway opened in 1836 and was the oldest independent railway company in the world. Its purpose was to carry slate through Snowdonia which could then be transported throughout the world. Slate suffered decline at about the same time as steam railways were coming to an end and closure of the line was inevitable. However, by the 1980s the railway was up and running again, this time with a completely different cargo. Restoration was underway, long before that in 1954 when dedicated volunteers began rebuilding and The Ffestiniog Railway Society is still valuable today in keeping the railway alive.

In Shropshire, the town of Bridgnorth has an old Bridgnorth High Town with its wonderful views of the River Severn Valley. From here, a bridge leads to the much visited Severn Valley Railway. The railway has a full-size standard gauge line which regularly runs passenger trains between Bridgnorth and Kidderminster in Worcestershire over a distance of 16 miles. The railway closely follows the river valley and crosses the River Severn via Victoria Bridge with its 200-feet single span. The visitors' centre in the Engine House at Highley has a reserve collection of steam locomotives and many exhibitions.

The Lines

GWR

Great Western Railway (GWR) was a remarkable feat of engineering which linked the West Country with South Wales and London. Founded in 1833, GWR was also known as "God's Wonderful Railway" and the "Great Way Round".

In 1835 the legendary Isambard Kingdom Brunel was appointed chief engineer of GWR. By the age of 27 after studying the entire route between Bristol and London, Brunel decided that the line should not pass through any major towns or cities and should adopt the broad gauge track, to allow for larger wheels, which would give a smoother ride at high speeds.

Over the next 22 years, GWR merged with a number of new railway lines of which many operated on standard gauge tracks. The different widths in the gauges often made travelling difficult for passengers, who had to change trains many times on a single journey. The dispute between broad and standard gauge was eventually solved by Midland Railway who built a third track which allowed both standard and broad gauge locomotives to run on the same line.

Brunel's Royal Albert Bridge, which was built in 1859, ran over the River Tamar linking Plymouth in Devon to Saltash in Cornwall. Also known as a bowstring suspension bridge it helped

■ **TOP:** Brunel's Royal Albert Bridge at Saltash.

■ **ABOVE:** A mixed gauge bulk road crossover.

By 1900 new locomotives including the Saint Class and Star Class were being introduced to the railway network and all broad gauge tracks were replaced with standard gauge.

In 1923 GWR was one of the only railway companies to maintain its identity at the end of the First World War after the government decided to amalgamate all UK railways into four main groups. As a result GWR managed to gain over 1,000 miles of new line with the companies that it was merged with giving the network almost 4,000 miles worth of line at this time.

On 1 January 1948 GWR was nationalised and became part of British Railways. In the early 1990s British Rail was privatised. The GWR name was revived by Great Western Trains, which operated on the old GWR lines between the South West of England and South Wales. The company is now known as First Great Western and some of the historic GWR structures can still be seen around the railway network to this day.

■ **ABOVE LEFT:** GWR locomotive 5029 "Nunney Castle".

■ **ABOVE:** Brunel and model of "The Iron Duke".

■ **BELOW INSET:** Station Master's office at Paddington.

37

GWR extend their lines into South Devon and through to Cornwall, eventually reaching Penzance in 1867. Brunel was renowned for his practical way of problem solving and designed his bridge to be simple, yet graceful. The bridge is comprised of an iron arch, hung by suspension chains on each side of the tube. The railway itself is carried on a plate girder road and the bridge is unique even today as it is the only suspension bridge of its kind to carry mainline trains.

By 1873 work on the Severn Tunnel had begun which allowed for a more direct route, linking South Gloucestershire in the West of England to Monmouthshire in South Wales. The tunnel passed under the estuary of the River Severn but after construction proved difficult and expensive the tunnel remained unopened until 1886.

■ **ABOVE:** "The Dominion of Canada", LNER A4 Class.

LNER

The London and North Eastern Railway (LNER) was the second largest of the "big four" railway companies (GWR, LMS and SR). It was most famous for its prestigious high-speed trains, along with the transportation of coal from North East England. Railway lines varied from the flat agricultural land of East Anglia, to the severe curves and gradients of Scotland and the Pennines.

Sir Ralph Wedgwood was the first chief general manager of LNER after the company was formed in 1923. Wedgwood developed a huge love for the railway from an early age and began working for North Eastern Railway (NER). He soon became district superintendent and then secretary in 1904. After he had served throughout the First World War, Wedgwood eventually returned to NER after spending three more years in the military. After becoming general manager of NER in 1922, he became chief general manager

of LNER in 1923. Wedgwood was an inspiring leader who had always remembered his early love for the railways. With this, Wedgwood made LNER a very successful company for its time.

After Wedgwood retired in the late 1930s he was approached by the government to become part of the Railway Executive Committee and to manage the railway networks across the UK.

With initial help from Wedgwood, LNER continued to prosper. It was made up of the Great Central Railway, Great Eastern Railway, Great Northern Railway, Great North of Scotland Railway, Hull and Barnsley Railway, North British Railway and North Eastern Railway. In total LNER owned over 7,000 miles worth of railway line, along with more than 7,600 locomotives, 20,000 coaches, 30,000 freight cars, 140 electric rolling stock and 10 rail cars.

Sir Nigel Gresley was a personal friend of Sir Ralph Wedgwood. Gresley helped produce many successful locomotives, which

■ **ABOVE:** T2 Class 63395 at Grosmont on the North Yorkshire Railway.

were known for their outstanding performance. He had previously worked for Great Northern Railway (GNR) and designed some of the most famous locomotives in the UK, which included the Flying Scotsman and the Mallard. Both of these trains were built to be incredibly fast and – despite the City of Truro locomotive claiming to have broken the 100mph speed record in 1904 – the Flying Scotsman was the first train to officially be recorded travelling at more than 100mph.

Arthur Peppercorn was a great admirer of Gresley and was another important designer for LNER. He spent only 18 months with the company but during his time he helped bring in the express passenger locomotive A1 and A2 Pacific Classes.

LNER was nationalised in 1948 along with the rest of the railways in the UK under the Transport Act of 1947 becoming part of British Railways. For years LNER was known to be the second largest of the "big four" railway companies in terms of route miles, but it was also the poorest. After British Railways was privatised in 1994 the East Coast Main Line was taken over and renamed Great North Eastern Railways (GNER).

LMS

The London Midland and Scottish Railway (LMS) was formed on 1 January 1923 as part of the Railways Act of 1921. It was an amalgamation of a number of railways including the Caledonian Railway, Glasgow and South Western Railway, Furness Railway, Highland Railway, London and North Western Railway, Midland Railway and North Staffordshire Railway.

Josiah Stamp was the first president of LMS in 1926. He had previously worked for the Inland Revenue while studying for his degree in economics. However, Stamp was not a railway man and he failed to see that LMS depended a great deal on its staff and their commitment and dedication, which was key to the success of the company up to that point.

Stamp appointed William Stanier as chief mechanical engineer of LMS in 1933 after a great deal of conflict within the company. Stanier had a long railway history after following his father into a career with GWR in Swindon. There he worked on a number of locomotives as a draughtsman before becoming an inspector of materials in 1900. Stamp may not have understood the range of management skills needed to help run his railway but he did understand the need for professional help when he asked Stanier to join LMS from GWR. Stanier was quickly put to work and soon brought about an important turning point in LMS locomotive design. Midland's small engine policy had come to an end and over the next eight years, Stanier was to reintroduce most of the LMS "first string" locomotives. He focused on introducing new ideas rather than continuing with the company's internal conflict.

Before becoming a part of LMS the Caledonian line was a major Scottish railway. It had operated for over 100 years and linked Glasgow and Edinburgh with lines to England.

Traditionally Scottish railways were not connected to lines in England and this often meant passengers had to endure long journeys by sea and rail. The Caledonian Railway was a big step forward and when it eventually opened in 1849 it took just over 12 hours to travel between London and Glasgow.

The North Staffordshire Railway (NSR) became part of the LMS group in 1923. The company was made up of smaller railway networks including the Derby and Crewe Railway along with the Macclesfield to Crewe and Harecastle to Sandbach lines.

Like a number of other railway companies that were taken over by the "big four" and then nationalised by British Railways, NSR suffered many closures during the 1960s and 1970s. This was due to the government beginning to modernise all railways across the UK.

By 1938 LMS operated over 6,800 miles of railway and was the largest of the "big four" railway companies operating in all parts of England,

Scotland, Ireland and Wales. On 1 January 1948 LMS, along with the other railway companies, was nationalised becoming part of British Railways. From the 1960s onwards many former LMS and other railway networks across the UK were closed and developed to support the latest 125mph inter-city train services.

■ **BELOW:** Monsal Head Viaduct built in 1867 for the Midland Railway.

Southern

Southern Railway (SR) was first introduced as a result of the Railways Act of 1921. It was formed to link London with South West England, Kent and the Channel ports, which spanned over a total of 2,186 miles.

Competition from newer modes of transport including cars and particularly buses were putting direct pressure on railway companies throughout the 1920s and early 1930s. GWR was hit very hard when the Western National Omnibus Company began operating in their region. A number of branch lines and mainline stations were forced to close as a result.

With the outbreak of the Second World War in 1939 all railways across the UK came under government control. Southern Railway was particularly active during the war and many branch lines were once again reopened. Both London and Plymouth were regular targets for German bombers and with the threat of a

German invasion on the south coast in 1940, the railway traffic to the Channel ports and the West Country were dominated with British troops.

After the war, Southern Railway along with the rest of the railway network was nationalised in 1948 and merged into British Railways. Many of the lines between London and Kent were damaged during the war as well as their trains and carriages.

The transport company Govia, which also owns neighbouring train company Southeastern, currently owns Southern Railway. The railway line was originally named Southern Railway Ltd before being branded Southern once again on 30 May 2004. The modern Southern trains can be seen today with their distinctive rounded logo with "Southern" written in yellow over a green bar.

■ **ABOVE:** Military ambulance train, 1949.

■ **BELOW:** Waterloo Station open in 1848 for the London and South Western Railway.

Settle & Carlisle

The Settle – Carlisle Railway was one of the engineering marvels of the Victorian age. It was completed in 1876 and travels 72 miles between Settle and Carlisle using 20 viaducts and 14 tunnels. Approximately 6,000 men worked on the line, which proved to be the last major railway in England to be constructed almost entirely by hand. The line was opened on 1 May 1876 and has survived two closure attempts in the 1960s and 1980s. Both of these attempts caused national outrage and in 1989 it was declared that the line would stay open after the public's support and increase in passenger numbers.

The Settle – Carlisle Railway has stood the test of time and overcome a number of problems. After nearly a century of minor use in the 1960s, the line's smaller stations were forced to close in 1970 and stopping passenger services were lowered to just two a day.

A lack of investment hindered the line until the 1980s. The majority of freight traffic was diverted onto the West Coast Main Line. The lack of maintenance meant that many of the line's viaducts and tunnels began to deteriorate. British Rail decided that it would cost too much money to renew the service and in 1984 closure notices were posted to all of the line's stations. However, the local authorities and rail enthusiasts campaigned to save the line and discovered that British Rail had unfairly neglected the line by diverting traffic to other routes and exaggerating repair costs. In 1989 they eventually agreed to keep the line open and to repair the viaducts and tunnels.

The line is still open and is considered one of the most scenic railway journeys in England. The service today comprises of mainly modern diesel and freight trains with the occasional charter steam engine. The freight trains are predominantly coal from Scotland travelling to Yorkshire power stations.

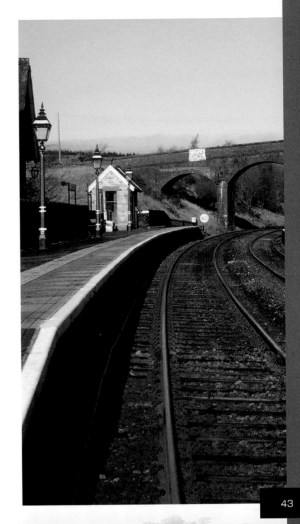

Classic Trains

CHELTENHAM FLYER

29P

It wasn't just the age of steam that was a phenomena across the globe during its heyday. The engines themselves had a pretty big part to play in capturing peoples' hearts as well, and over the next few pages, we take a look at some of the world's iconic engines and the part they played in the past and where they are today. From Stephenson's Rocket, the Duchess of Hamilton, Evening Star and the City of Truro, to many others, both in the UK and further afield, these classic engines were an essential component in the rise of the steam age. But sadly, they were also fairly instrumental in the demise of steam with rising costs, increased

■ **ABOVE:** "Golden Arrow".

maintenance, back-breaking work and unreliability. The way these engines worked, however, is fascinating and many were fitted with a piston steam engine which was double acting on account of the valve allowing high pressure steam to act alternatively on both faces of the piston.

The slide valve was responsible for letting the high pressure steam into either side of the cylinder where the control rod for the valve was usually hooked into a linkage attached to a cross-head. This enabled the cross-head to slide the valve as well and for a locomotive, it meant that the engineer could put the engine into reverse. The exhaust steam was simply allowed to vent outwards

which is why so much water was an integral part of the process because so much of it was lost in the exhaust steam. This exhaust steam also accounts for the noise that steam locomotives make – when the valve opens the cylinder to release the steam, it escapes under huge

amounts of pressure and gives a loud noise – passengers were certainly aware the train was at the station, or on its way. The piston itself moves extremely slowly as the engine first pulls away and it is this action that gives off the rhythmical noise as the engine starts to quicken in time with the piston. The cross-head is linked to a drive rod which in turn links to coupling rods which drive the wheels. It is the coupling rods that enable the wheels to turn in unison.

The boiler in the engine is responsible for heating the water to create the steam and there were two types available: fire tube and water tube boilers. During the 1800s, the fire tube assembly was more widely used, but if pressure became too great, then a major explosion could ensue. Today, however, in preserved locomotives, water tube boilers are more common and water runs through a rack of tubes which are positioned into the hot elements of the fire and the overall aim is for the boiler to extract all possible heat from the source to improve efficiency.

■ **BELOW:** "Tornado" pulls "Mallard" along the East Coast Main Line.

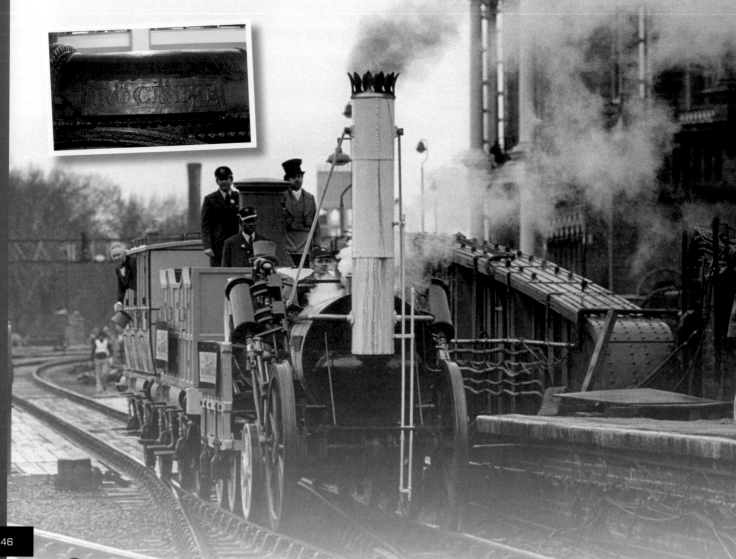

George Stephenson's Rocket

In 1829, George Stephenson, with the help of his son Robert and Henry Booth built the early steam locomotive, known as the Rocket at the Forth Street Works in Newcastle-upon-Tyne.

Although the Rocket was not the first steam locomotive to be built, it was the first to adopt several new design features. Early locomotives had consisted of a single pipe surrounded by water whereas the Rocket with its multi-tube design had 25 copper tubes running the length of the boiler, which allowed the hot gases to be carried from the firebox. Also with its blast pipe increasing the draught to the fire by concentrating the exhaust steam at the base of the chimney, the Rocket was able to go faster than any of its rivals.

This Rocket had been built for the 1829 Rainhill Trials, which were held by the Liverpool and Manchester Railway Company to find the best locomotive engine of the time. During the race the locomotives had to travel 20 laps of the course and the Rocket reached speeds of 24mph. Some 15,000 people are reported to have come along to see the race between these locomotives.

On 15 September 1830, at the opening ceremony of the Liverpool and Manchester Railway which attracted numerous people from government and industry – including the Prime Minister the Duke of Wellington – William Huskisson, the local Member of Parliament for Liverpool, was injured (and later died) after being struck by the Rocket.

In 1834 modifications were made to the Rocket when it was selected to test a newly developed rotary steam engine designed by Lord Dundonald. Following this modification, which involved removing the Rocket's cylinders and driving rods so that the engines could be installed directly onto the driving axle at a cost of £80, an operational trial was carried out on 22 October 1934 but this modification gave disappointing results.

In 1862 the Rocket was donated to the Patent Office Museum in London and it is still kept there to this day.

Sir Nigel Gresley

Born on 19 June 1876, Sir Nigel Gresley was one of LNER's most famous locomotive designers. At the start of his career he worked under engineer J A F Aspinall on the Lancashire and Yorkshire Railway (L&YR) in 1898. After working as a foreman in the running sheds for many years he became an assistant superintendent in 1904. He stayed with L&YR for another year before resigning at the age of 29 to become superintendent of GNR's Carriage and Wagon Department.

By 1911 Gresley had become chief mechanical engineer of GNR. He began designing a number of innovative locomotives and by 1922 his first three-cylinder Pacific (A1 Class) Great Northern was built.

Sir Ralph Wedgwood approached the young Gresley in 1923 and offered him the position of LNER's chief mechanical engineer. Gresley began work with LNER almost immediately and started introducing some new engine policies to the company. Gresley wanted to bring back the larger locomotives, which were better suited for the mainline services. He also opted to stay with his well-tested and established designs which would prove an important money saver as LNER was the poorest of the "big four" railway companies.

Gresley soon became one of the UK's most famous locomotive designers. After starting with the Pacific A1 Class this was later developed by LNER and upgraded to the A3, which included the iconic Flying Scotsman. The more streamlined A4 Classes were to follow which included the Mallard, which to this day holds the world record as the fastest steam locomotive. Many of Gresley's later locomotive designs took a great deal of influence from his early Pacific A1 Class designs.

Sir Nigel Gresley was knighted in 1936 for his life long dedication to locomotive design. He died on 5 April 1941 and is buried in Netherseal, Derbyshire.

Evening Star

The Evening Star was built at the Crewe and Swindon works in 1960 and was the last ever steam locomotive to be built and run on British railways. The Evening Star was the only locomotive in its class to be given a name and unlike any of the other members of its class that were painted black, the Evening Star was painted green and had a double chimney that was copper-capped.

Robert Riddles was in charge of the 9F design, which would later influence the design of the Evening Star locomotive. The 9F was introduced between 1954 and 1960 after Riddles had argued that the 2-10-0 wheel configuration was best suited for this locomotive. During the Second World War he developed a 2-10-0 design with a wide firebox, eventually seeing 150 being built of which 25 were bought by British Railways. The Germans and French had also built and experimented with the 2-10-0 models since 1915.

There was a great deal of scepticism over the 9F design and many critics wanted to see a new 2-8-2 engine built instead. This would have had a number of advantages as it could use many of the components from the earlier Class 7 4-6-2 Britannia. Despite the opposition, Riddles pushed forward his 2-10-0 designs in July 1951.

The first 9F was launched in January 1954 after a number of years' delay due to a national steel shortage. The 9F began well but was not without its problems. Reports soon arose that drivers were having difficulties closing the regulator, which was indeed a major problem. The prospect of a runaway train was becoming very possible. One example of this close call was when a 9F was travelling down from Ebbw Vale and its drivers were unable to close its regulator for several miles.

Luckily they managed to slow the train and went on without incident.

Calls were made from all over the UK for the regulators on all 9F locomotives to be changed. The 9F was modified and experienced no further problems. Soon it was being used on many different routes across the country and was ordered right up until 1957 when British Railways decided to phase out steam locomotives.

9Fs were specially built for services on the London Midland, Eastern, Western and North Eastern regions. Many of the first of these locomotives were reluctantly received in the Western region after their experience of its earlier problems.

The Evening Star was modified from the 9F and introduced in 1960. Despite this it had a rather short life span. An accident involving Evening Star had greatly contributed to the steam locomotive's withdrawal from service in 1965. It was also facing

increased competition from new diesel locomotives. Even so, the original 9F was one of the best steam locomotive designs that was ever built and was highly effective for the heavy loads for which it was designed to carry.

Today there are nine surviving 9F locomotives of which one is the Evening Star and it can be seen on display at the National Railway Museum in York along with another surviving 9F locomotive, the Black Prince. This model was built a year before the Evening Star in 1959. The Black Prince was in service for nine years working for British Railways as a heavy iron ore train from Liverpool Docks to Shotton Steelworks; it was the last steam locomotive to haul iron ore from the docks in 1967 before the newer diesel locomotives began to take over.

Duchess of Hamilton

The Duchess of Hamilton was a new streamlined locomotive built in Crewe during 1938. The demand for extra power to the Duchess Class 4-6-2 led William Stanier at LMS to develop the Princess Royal Class, enlarging the boiler and modifying the chassis. A total of 38 Duchess locomotive engines were built between 1937 and 1948.

The first five Duchess locomotives were painted blue with four silver stripes to match the coach livery of the Coronation Scot train. All Duchess locomotives were named after the Coronation, five were named after royalty, 10 after duchesses, 21 after cities served by LMS and one other after designer William Stanier. After the Coronation locomotives, the next five were streamlined and painted red in order to match new rolling stock.

However, the streamlining of these engines was halted in 1946 after companies found that it was having very little effect on the locomotive's performance while travelling below 90mph. The casing was also rather unpopular with railway maintenance staff and by 1949 most locomotives had been stripped of this design.

The first locomotive of the Duchess Class was to be built for the Coronation in 1937 followed by the Queen Elizabeth, the Queen Mary, the Princess Alice and the Princess Alexandra. A year later came the Duchess of Gloucester and the Duchess of Norfolk followed by the Duchess of Devonshire, the Duchess of Rutland and then the Duchess of Hamilton. The Duchess of Buccleuch was also a 1938 locomotive as was the Duchess of Atholl, the Duchess of Montrose, the Duchess of Sutherland and the Duchess of Abercorn. Today there are only

six Duchess locomotives that have been preserved, one of which is the Duchess of Hamilton, which is now based in York.

After the Duchess of Hamilton was selected for the Coronation Scot tour of North America in 1939, it was temporarily known as the No. 6220 Coronation for this trip. It covered 3,121 miles of North America and visited 38 towns and cities ending at the World Fair in New York. The outbreak of the Second World War prevented it from returning to the UK until 1943 where it resumed its identity as the Duchess of Hamilton once again and served on the London Midland Region of British Railways until it was withdrawn in 1964.

The Duchess of Hamilton was built as an express locomotive and had a very modern and streamlined look for its time. The Duchess Class was certainly renowned for being one of the fastest locomotives in service

in the UK. The Princess Coronation Class trains were the most powerful express passenger locomotives used in the UK working on the West Coast Main Line for LMS.

A decision to restore the Duchess of Hamilton to the engine's original appearance with its streamlined casing was announced by the National Railway Museum in York in 2005. Work was completed in 2007 to coincide with the 70th anniversary of the Coronation Scot service for which the locomotive was originally built.

The Duchess of Hamilton was the 10th in its class to be built and today is a preserved steam locomotive, which until 2005 was sited at the National Railway Museum in York along with the Duchess of Sutherland and the City of Birmingham, which are also both preserved duchesses locomotives. Billy Butlin saved the train from the breaker's yard in Barry, South Wales, when he purchased the locomotive to become a playground attraction at one of his holiday camps where it survived before being loaned to the National Railway Museum by Butlins for 20 years from 1976. However, the museum purchased the Duchess in 1987 and the train left service in 1996 when its licence finally expired.

City of Truro

The Swindon-built locomotive the City of Truro, is famous for being the first locomotive to pass the speed of 100mph. On 9 May 1904 not only did it reach this speed but it was also the first vehicle of any kind to do so. The City of Truro was one of 20 City Class locomotives from GWR and had built up a well-known reputation for its speed.

On 9 May 1904 the City of Truro was used to collect a cargo of "ocean mails", which had arrived from San Francisco on a steamer bound for Plymouth. On board there were about 1,300 large bags of mail, which were packed into five eight-wheeled postal vans plus a large, sorting van. Also carried on this run was a payment by the Americans to the French for work on the Panama Canal. This load was estimated to weigh around 148 tons, not including the locomotive and tender which weighed around another 90 tons.

The journey began at 9.23 am and for the first two hours the City of Truro reached an average speed of 62mph. However, just west of Taunton, Charles Rous-Marten the journey's timekeeper recorded a top speed of 102.3mph. Great Western Railways were sensitive about admitting this record initially as feelings were running high following the derailment of a night tourist train at Preston.

It was not until December 1907, a whole three and a half years later, that *The Railway Magazine* finally published a table of maximum speeds recorded for various classes of locomotive where this feat was recorded. It was another 14 years before GWR officially laid claim to this record by which time the validity of the timings were being questioned.

Built in 1903 the City of Truro had quite a short working life for a locomotive after it was taken out of service in 1931. From 1931 to 1957 the City of Truro was put on view at the National Railway Museum in York on static display. From 1962 until 1984 it was moved to the GWR Museum in Swindon and then restored for the GWR's 150th anniversary celebrations. After this it was returned to the National Railway Museum and occasionally used on mainline outings.

of different uses across the railway network being used from Bournemouth all the way to Wick. They were quickly seen running express and stopping passenger services as well as fast freights to mine workings in the Ayrshire coalfield. These jobs could have arguably been done more effectively by a heavier freight locomotive but the Black 5 was very versatile and was used relentlessly, including over summer weekends to haul excursions and freight cargo.

The last Black 5 locomotives were to be some of the best-produced models. Its appearance was much different to earlier class designs, however underneath it was still similar to the traditional Class 5 but with a great deal of added equipment.

Despite these new improvements the Black 5 could not withstand the innovation of the new diesel and electric engines. It was beginning to be withdrawn from service in 1961 and had completely halted by 1968. Eighteen of these locomotives have been preserved and are still ever popular with enthusiasts around the world.

Stanier Black 5

Sir William Stanier's Black 5 was one of the most successful locomotives of all time. The Black 5 was first introduced on the London, Midland and Scottish Railway (LMSR) in 1934. It was built as a response to the growing demand for a locomotive that could be fast enough for passenger travel and yet strong enough for express freight duties. The Black 5 was a very capable locomotive and did everything that was asked of it.

The Stanier Class 5 4-6-0, also known as the Black 5, was produced between 1934 and 1951. Over this time 842 were built, many with a cheap government loan, which was used to generate employment during the depression of the 1930s.

As the Black 5 increased in numbers they found a variety

Flying Scotsman

Some people would have no qualms in stating that the Flying Scotsman is the most iconic steam locomotive of all time due to its lengthy journey of 390 miles between London and Edinburgh, which initially took more than 10 hours in total. Today the same journey would take less than half the time compared to the journey time of the Flying Scotsman, which started boarding passengers in the early 1900s.

In 1924 all British railways were grouped under the Railway Grouping Act. This act was passed by the government of the time in order to stem the losses being made by a large portion of the 120 railway companies and aimed to move the railways away from internal competition. They wanted to retain some of the benefits, which the country had derived from the largely government controlled railway during the First World War. This act created the "big four" railway companies (GWR, LMS, LNER and SR) replacing the numerous other railway companies that previously existed.

The Flying Scotsman or the Special Scotch Express as it was known, became the flagship brand of LNER who had a more powerful marketing dynamic compared to the

other three railway companies. The Flying Scotsman was proven to be a good investment for LNER as the economic depression of the 1930s was especially difficult; it kept them in business by travelling non-stop between the two cities of London and Edinburgh, cutting its journey time from more than 10 hours to 7 hours and 20 minutes. By the end of the depression, passengers were being treated to luxuries such as an on board hairdressing service, cocktail bar and fine cuisine. Even today, the Flying Scotsman is still the most talked about train on the East Coast Main Line. GNER were as keen to promote their flagship locomotive as LNER were all those years before them.

At a cost of £7,945, the Flying Scotsman originally went on display at Marylebone before beginning its 80-year service as No. 1472. After being repaired in 1924 the train was renumbered No. 4472 and with the help of chief mechanical engineer, Nigel Gresley, it managed to run non-stop from London to Edinburgh on one tender of coal. Gresley was largely responsible for the Flying Scotsman's outstanding performance and the train was so popular that it was used in the film *The Flying Scotsman* in 1929.

With the outbreak of the Second World War the Flying Scotsman was mainly used to pull goods, parcels and transport passengers during the war years. British Railways recovered from the war and restored full service

again in 1948 but unfortunately for the Flying Scotsman there was no need for it to continue its service as a leading light of the railways. After recommendations from Dr Richard Beeching's report on behalf of the government, the Flying Scotsman was due to finish service and be scrapped in 1955. Not everyone felt that this should be the end for this steam locomotive and quick thinking businessman and member of the Eastern Regional Board for British Railways, Alan Pegler, bought the Flying Scotsman for £3,000 in 1963. He set about giving it a complete overhaul and restored it to its former glory. Pegler took the locomotive on tour in the US before the Flying Scotsman was bought by William McAlpine and shipped back to the UK. In 1988 the locomotive was on tour again, this time in Australia where it established the record for the longest non-stop run by a steam locomotive at 442 miles.

Despite this record the Flying Scotsman will always be most famous for its many journeys

between London and Edinburgh, which opened up so many opportunities for people to travel the length of the country. The line itself was built by three separate railway companies in the Victorian period. The first section between London and Doncaster was constructed by Great Northern Railway which was finished in 1853 but, it took the North Eastern Railway another 23 years to finish the next stretch of line between Doncaster and Berwick. The final section of the line was finished first by the North British Railway from Berwick to Edinburgh in 1846. A terminus was built at York within the city walls and locomotives, whether travelling north or south, were required to reverse into the original station. A newly built station helped relieve the problem in 1877; however, trains were faced with the same issue at Newcastle station as the site in the city was also built as a terminus. The problem was solved with the King Edward VII Bridge built in 1906. The line remained pretty much as it was built originally except

for the 13-mile diversion to avoid subsidence over an active mining area, which was constructed around Selby coalfield in 1983. Today GNER operates the line.

Service began for the Flying Scotsman in 1923, which ran exclusively for first- and second-class ticket holders at 10am every day. More than 25 years later, the Flying Scotsman became accessible to the wider public when third-class tickets were introduced. Many other rival companies were trying to offer a much faster service than the famous locomotive. The Flying Scotsman managed to reduce its journey time to less than eight hours by not stopping in York, which it had been doing on previous trips. There was a constant drive to find ways to reduce its journey time and some were proved successful. The Flying Scotsman is now located at the National Railway Museum in York who are in the process of restoring the locomotive so that it may once more grace the East Coast Main Line again.

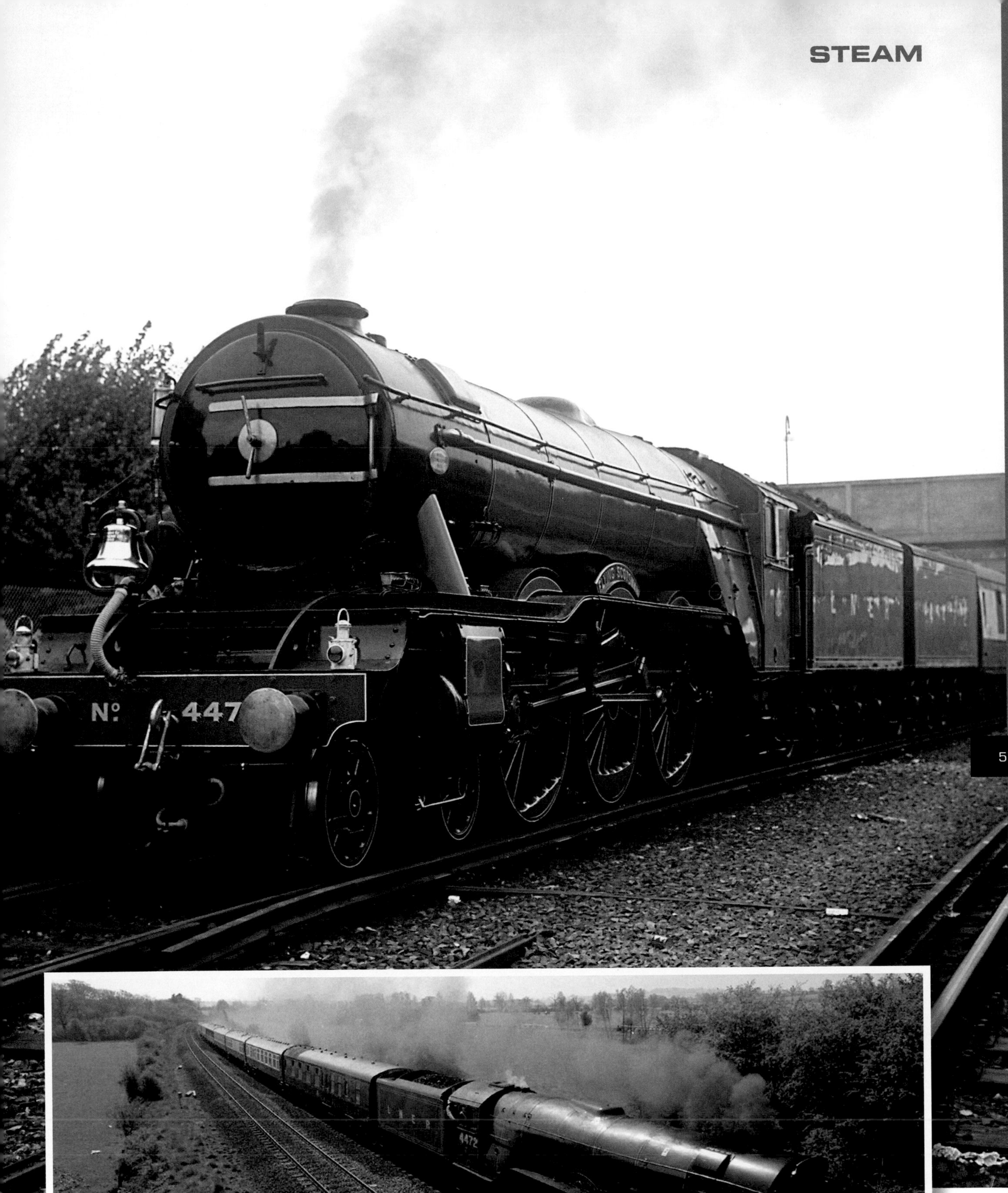
Nº 447

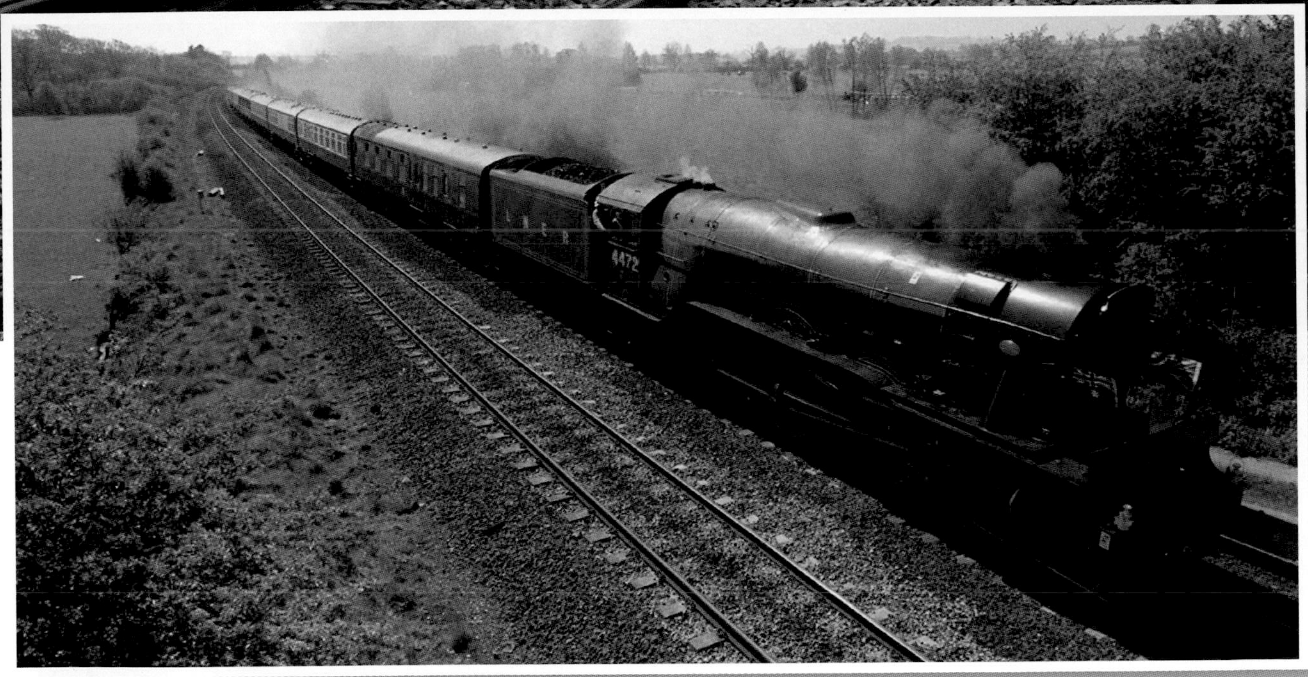
4472

Mallard

The A4 Class 4-6-2 Mallard broke the world rail speed record on 3 July 1938 reaching a speed of 126mph, which is a feat no other steam locomotive has ever been able to match. The Mallard's double kylchap blast pipe gave it improved steaming and an extra turn of speed that made it faster than any single chimney A4 Class locomotives at that time.

The record-breaking No. 4468 Mallard had only been in service three months when designer, Sir Nigel Gresley, approved it for this famous record-breaking run. Mallard driver Joe Duddington took the locomotive south through Grantham and accelerated up to Stoke summit. The next 20 miles of the journey was largely downhill and Duddington gave the engine as much power as he could muster. Four minutes later the speed record belonged to Mallard which reached 120mph but it was to go even faster finally reaching the speed of 126mph. Later on in the run the Mallard developed engine problems due to overheating and it was forced to crawl back to Doncaster but no steam engine would ever go faster.

Locomotives throughout Europe and the US, including the diesel-electric "Fliegende Hamburger" of the German State Railways and the "Burlington Zephyr" from the US were beginning to make many UK steam locomotives appear dated and slow. Gresley therefore decided to begin working on streamlining his

latest A3 Class designs. The A3s had originally been more reliable than some of Gresley's other designs, but something more streamlined was now required to compete with the headlines that trains overseas were receiving. The Flying Scotsman, the engineer's A1 Class design had reached 100mph during trials while his Papyrus A3 locomotive was said to have achieved 108mph.

Gresley was therefore summoned by LNER to take his streamlining ideas and put them into practice.

After a number of long trials involving wind tunnel testing he finally came up with the iconic A4 Class. There was a great deal of criticism over the way in which Gresley was adapting his design, but he managed to streamline almost every part of the locomotive both inside and out. The casing was worked, the steam passages were streamlined and the boiler pressure was increased from 220 psi to 250 psi. Further modifications based on the A3 were made and the inaugural

run of this new "super-powered" steam locomotive was held on 27 September 1935 when the train travelled from London Kings Cross to Grantham reaching a speed of 112mph. The crew were unaware of this record-breaking speed and Gresley had to inform them that they were making the passengers nervous after which the train slowed to a more moderate speed.

The Mallard first officially came into service in early 1938. Three further locomotives were built to run in conjunction with the formative engine on the new Silver Jubilee service to Newcastle upon Tyne. The speed of the new A4 Class engines began to cut journey times between Newcastle and London down to four hours and the route was a huge success with both LNER and passengers alike. New services were introduced and extended prompting LNER to produce even more A4s to help cope with the increasing demand. The UK's first inter-city network was born when these remarkable train services were then extended to Leeds and Bradford.

Other engineers were soon attempting to copy Gresley's streamlined locomotive design and it wasn't long before railway companies such as LMS introduced the Coronation Class and Southern Railways announced a new streamlined class both of which were

trying to better the Mallard's speed record. Many railway bosses were becoming increasingly concerned about passenger safety and an agreement was soon reached to put safety first and to ensure slower

speeds had to be reached.

The Mallard was named by Gresley who came up with its name while he was out feeding the ducks. It cost LNER almost £8,500 to produce. Gresley, chief mechanical

engineer at LNER for most of his working life, built the locomotive in Doncaster in the early 1930s. LNER, like many other railway companies were facing increasing competition from new methods of transport including cars but mainly buses which increased the pressure on engineers such as Gresley to design much faster, more reliable locomotives and carriages.

With the modernisation of British Railways during the 1960s, the A4 Class was beginning to be phased out across the country. In 1962 it was announced that the A4s were to be scrapped and the last A4 withdrew from service in 1966.

The Mallard was taken out of service in 1963 having covered a staggering one and a half million miles over its lifespan. It was saved from being scrapped in the 1960s and was fully restored to its working

order in 1980. In early 1987 the Mallard was taken on a couple of runs between York and Leeds. On 5 July 2008, it was allowed to be seen outside for the first time in years to

be displayed alongside her A4 sisters, reuniting all four of the remaining A4s preserved in the UK. It is now proudly on display at the National Railway Museum in York.

Tornado

The Tornado is a recent mainline steam locomotive that was built in Darlington, England between 1994 and 2008. It was the first such locomotive to be built in the UK since the Evening Star in 1960. Named after the Panavia Tornado combat aircraft, the locomotive is set to run on the UK rail network and mainline connected heritage railways.

The A1 Steam Locomotive Trust, which is a charitable trust that was founded in 1990, drew up plans to build the Tornado. Their aim was to build the Tornado and then potentially other locomotives in the future. The Tornado is a direct descendent of the LNER Peppercorn A1 Class.

Arthur Peppercorn who was the last chief mechanical engineer of LNER originally designed the A1 locomotive. Peppercorn was born on 29 January 1889 in Stoke Prior in Herefordshire. Like Sir Nigel Gresley, Peppercorn was the son of a clergyman who hoped his son would follow him into the church. However, Peppercorn dreamt of becoming a steam engine driver from an early age. After spending a lot of his time on the railways, Peppercorn expressed his desire to move to Doncaster to further his career. Peppercorn or "Pepp" as he was known came to Doncaster as an apprentice training under Henry Ivatt in 1905, the same year as Nigel Gresley came to GNR from the Lancashire and Yorkshire Railway, as Carriage and Wagon superintendent. Peppercorn worked with GNR for many years before moving to LNER where he worked for around 18 months. Even though he only spent a very short time with the company he managed to design the express famous passenger locomotive A1 and A2 Pacific Classes.

By September 1945 Peppercorn's predecessor, Edward Thompson, revealed plans to rebuild one of Gresley's first Pacific classes, 4470 Great Northern at Doncaster Works. It wasn't just the locomotive's new Royal blue livery lined out in red that was striking but there was also very little remaining of the original locomotive design. The new Great Northern locomotive was a rather angular looking locomotive. Despite it having a number of problems, Thompson was satisfied with his A1 Class and placed an order for 16 locomotives to be built in October 1945 and then another 23 in 1946. But, these locomotives would later

62

emerge as the Peppercorn A1s, after being further modified from Thompson's original design. The first A1, No. 60114, appeared from Doncaster in August 1948 and was named W P Allen.

Some of the first Gresley Pacific locomotives were the most famous. These included the A3 4472 Flying Scotsman and A4 4468 Mallard, which were both three-cylinder machines and drove all cylinders onto the middle axle. Peppercorn, much like Thompson used divided drive, with the middle cylinder connected to the leading axle. But, unlike Thompson, Peppercorn used a slightly larger grate, which was much the same as that first used by Gresley on his iconic P2 2001 Cock O' the North.

The original Peppercorn A1 Class was built at Doncaster and Darlington,

after British Railways was nationalised in 1948. This type of locomotive was ideally suited for the post-war conditions, which typically led to poorer maintenance facilities and locomotives were forced to use lower grade coal than their predecessors. Some of the last A1s were even equipped with roller bearings which enabled them to run for an average of 118,000 miles between heavy

repairs, making them the cheapest to run of all British steam locomotives in the same category. They proved to be some of the most reliable express passenger steam locomotives owned by British Railways.

However, as it was with so many other steam locomotives at the time, all A1s were eventually scrapped after an average life of only 15 years when new diesel engines were being

introduced during the 1960s.

Enthusiasts attempted to save the last, A1 60145 Saint Mungo, but unfortunately failed and it too was withdrawn and then scrapped in September 1966.

After being built the Tornado first ran on 29 July 2008 from Darlington and was put through a variety of operational tests. It was soon moved to the National Railway Museum in York. After being painted in the famous LNER Apple Green, it was approved as a mainline passenger locomotive and set out on its first commercial trip on 31 January 2009. In all, the Tornado cost around £3 million to build. It can be

expected to reach speeds of 100mph and would be the fastest steam locomotive in the UK.

The Tornado was featured on the television show, *Top Gear,* in 2009 as part of a three-way race between presenters Jeremy Clarkson, Richard Hammond and James May. In this race from London to Edinburgh the Tornado was racing against a 1949 Jaguar XK120 sports car and a 1949 Vincent Black Shadow motorcycle. The Tornado finished in second place to the Jaguar XK120 after it was forced to stop on occasion and even though it was capable of achieving 100mph, it was limited to around 75mph for the race.